BLESSED

ARE THE DEBONAIR:

THE WIT AND WISDOM OF

CHARLES E. S. KRAEMER

APRIL 25, 1909 - JUNE 23, 1988

COMPILED AND WRITTEN BY:
Ann Hartzog Hall
Bobbye and Wool Howell
Heath K. Rada

with editorial assistance from:
Charles L. Cornwell

PUBLISHED BY:
Guidelines Enterprise
Richmond, Virginia 23227

To

Beryl Birdsong Kraemer

Charles' beloved "Mimi,"

life-long companion, and helpmeet--

and to her family and many friends,

a grace-filled child of God.

It is sometimes wise to remember that there is such a thing as Christian nonchalance. Maybe there is room for a new beatitude: "Blessed are the debonair," in whom the Word of God sparkles with graciousness and charm.

--James T. Cleland,
The True and Lively Word

FOREWORD

Many years ago I met a man who helped to change my life. I had entered the Presbyterian School of Christian Education (then the General Assembly's Training School for Lay Workers) as a graduate student with a sense of call but anxious and uncertain about what that call meant for my life. In late summer I had determined to enroll, only to discover that all the available places were taken. So I called the president, and in a slow Texas drawl that was infectiously calming, he said, "You come on up here and I'll make room for you." And indeed he did, even to the point of helping me move into my room.

That man, the president of the school, was Dr. Charles E. S. Kraemer. He gave to me--and to all the students-- two critical gifts. One was a stronger sense of identity as a Christian and an understanding of what we, as Christians, need to do to live as faithful and obedient disciples. The other gift was seeing to it that we got an education second to none in equipping us with the tools to serve faithfully and well as directors of education, church musicians, and missionaries in America and throughout the world.

Charles taught us that as lay workers we had a calling to fulfill and hard work to do equally as important as the work of theologians, Biblical scholars, and those called to preaching and pastoral ministries. For those who wanted to serve without taking the route of ordination, he cleared a way. And in a patriarchal world he made a place for women.

Charles also taught us that we could get the job done with goodwill, with humor, with negotiation rather than

through battling, strife, and "win/lose" philosophy. Now a fierce sense of competition and a litigious attitude seem to prevail throughout the society--from business and sports to politics and personal relationships. There could not be a more propitious or providential time to remember Charles E. S. Kraemer, to introduce him to others, and to enjoy reading about a man who "moved mountains" with his extraordinary wit and wisdom. A man who caught you so powerfully with his simple and genuine humanity that you knew you were in the presence of a rare spirit.

Simply and powerfully he caught the four writers of this little volume. One of us as a teenager first knew the real life of the church as Charles moved into his pastorate in Charlotte. He was caught by seeing the old church come to life and by the one who seemed to engender this life. Two of us got caught soon after we entered what was then A.T.S. where he was first our president, then our instructor, and finally our friend for life. The fourth one was caught also as a student, but this connection was forged when he became president of the school Charles had served, by then known as P.S.C.E.

We do not intend for this book to be a biography in the usual sense of the word. We leave that task to others. We do, however, find it necessary to provide some context for most of the stories we tell, so bit by bit biographical details do emerge.

Rather than a chronological biography, we seek to capture in words the essence of the life and wisdom of the man all four of us were privileged to call friend and, in some small measure, fellow worker. Yet we freely admit at the outset that our task is an impossible one. How can you catch the essence of any living being on paper--especially of one so vitally alive as Charles? Throughout his

life his mind churned out profound wisdom and the witticisms to make the wisdom more palatable, never more so than when he struggled with Parkinson's disease.

We are indebted to him. We believe the church is indebted to him--particularly in the Southeastern United States where he worked and lived and witnessed as a Presbyterian. We hope that some measure of the man will be revealed in our endeavor so that those who knew him might be reminded anew of our debt to him. We also hope that those who did not know him might be introduced to his keen mind and probing intellect and come to acknowledge their debt to him as well.

The four of us are not the only ones who feel that Charles was an extraordinary presence. We are not the only ones who think something of his essence should be captured on paper. As soon as we undertook this project, we were surrounded by others who offered words of encouragement and support as well as their memories. To all of them, as well as to Charles himself, we are indebted. Their sharing and concern have made our task a joy.

We have compiled the material and written this book as a gift of love. In the process we have received far more love than we have given--from one another, from Charles and Beryl and their family, and from those of you who have encouraged us. We have worked hard. The fact that Kraemer stories and Kraemerisms circulate in different versions should not be surprising. A few of them may even be apocryphal. Early on, an oral tradition grew up around Charles and accompanied him throughout his life. We have sifted through many stories (and several versions of some of the stories) to find the best ones for this book. While we can vouch for the authenticity of most of them, we cannot guarantee every reader that the version we de-

cided to use is precisely the version he or she first heard or recounts to others with glee.

Throughout it all we have had an unbelievable amount of fun. Now it is time for us to lay down this project and turn the results over to you, the readers. May you also have fun!

--Ann Hartzog Hall

INTRODUCTION

To those seeing him for the first time, Charles Edgar Stanberry Kraemer--or simply Charles, as his beloved wife Beryl called him--was not an imposing physical presence. (Yet he played high school football and baseball!) But once in his actual presence, you were captivated first by his pleasant face and his gentle smile and then by his blue eyes, eyes that twinkled with a wry joy. In no time at all you were simply and powerfully caught by his unpretentious and genuine humanity as well as by his wisdom and wit. You knew you were encountering a child of God, meeting a brother for life.

Charles was born in Bonham, Texas, a small town in an area of blackland prairie just south of the Red River that marks the boundary between Texas and Oklahoma. He graduated from Davidson College and Louisville Theological Seminary. He did graduate work in counseling and served churches in Kentucky, Missouri, Mississippi, and North Carolina before being named president of what is now the Presbyterian School of Christian Education in Richmond, Virginia. He served as Moderator of the Presbyterian Church (U.S.). When he retired, he moved first to Davidson, North Carolina, and then to Charlotte, where he and Beryl and their oldest son Fred lived. There are two other children: Jane (Mrs. Paul B. Scott) of Kingsport, Tennessee, and Phil, of Norfolk, Virginia. Charles and Beryl have four grandchildren.

Perhaps the major key to the man is an understanding of his delightful sense of humor. He seems to have had an inbred sense of the ridiculous which bubbled to the surface

even in the most difficult of situations. He was able to share this and brought healing to many situations through humor.

In a letter to Ann Hall dated April 17, 1987, Charles commented on humor and his attempt to use it: "Karl Barth wrote, 'Humor is the opposite of self-admiration and self-praise.' A professor in my seminary days said to us that we could never take our calling too seriously, but we could take ourselves too seriously. When we are free to laugh at ourselves sometimes we are free to see what is funny about the situations we human beings get ourselves into. This kind of humor is not bitter or cynical, not the superficial spirit of carnival nor does it grow out of the feelings of superiority over other people."

Yet on another occasion, Charles told Ann of his reservations about this project, and then said, "...I do not want to be thought of as a clown. I like for people to laugh, but I like also to be thought of as deep and intellectual and theological."

None of us would deny the depth of the man. We hope it shows through our words. Without a keen mind and a deep faith, he could not have touched as many lives as profoundly as he did. He witnessed and ministered to inmates on death row as well as to young and growing people in the stimulating environment of an institution of higher education, to the old and dying as well as to young colleagues just starting their own ministries in the church. He ministered to street people and bank presidents with equal charm, depth, and elan. He was indeed a man of wit and wisdom who pushed himself, and all whom he met, to be the best they could be for their own satisfaction and for the glory of God.

THE EARLY YEARS

Anyone having no more than a nodding acquaintance with Charles Kraemer knew that he was from Bonham, Texas. It is no secret that small towns shape their sons and daughters in subtle ways as well as nurture them intensely and obviously. Sometimes their hold lasts a lifetime. For instance, recall the inauguration of James A. Jones as president of Union Theological Seminary in Virginia. Many presidents of institutions attended, and each one was asked to summarize his educational background and give his present position. There were full accounts of grand universities and prestigious seminaries. There were quite a few Ph.D.'s, D.D.'s, Th.D.'s., S.T.D.'s, and so on. When it came time for Charles to introduce himself, he stood up and said, "Charles Kraemer, Bonham High School, Bonham, Texas." Then he sat down.

Charles' father was held in great affection by those who knew him. Frederick Adolphus Kraemer was born in Little Rock, Arkansas. His family had come from Pennsylvania and Ohio. He was a railroad conductor and there is no doubt that Charles got much of his humor from his father. It is said that he brought home many tales from his train trips.

Harriet F. Phillips, Charles' mother, was born in Bonham after her parents and three sisters had moved there from Virginia. Except for one sister who became a schoolteacher, the other girls married and reared their families in Bonham. This made for an unusual closeness among them. Everyone shared in the sadness when Harriet and Fred's first son died at the age of two. Charles, their second son,

3

was born April 25, 1909. When he was eight years old, his sister Ann was born.

The story of how Charles was named gives a further glimpse into the nature of this small East Texas town. His parents' devotion and faithfulness to their Presbyterian Church was extended to their pastor, Edgar Williams. Their son was given the name Edgar. The paternal grandmother's family name was Stanberry, so Stanberry was added to Edgar. The Kraemers thought they had completed the naming process when Mr. Foster, who lived down the street, reminded them that they had promised to name a son after him. So Charles was put in front of the rest-- Charles Edgar Stanberry Kraemer. Mr. Foster, a photographer, made Charles' picture every year. Charles' father quipped on numerous occasions that he wished he had named his son for the local grocer!

The Christmas Nativity scenes in Bonham must have been something to remember. Nearing the Christmas season one year Charles reported to a buddy that it was "time to get out the bathrobes and the excelsior."

The Kraemer family loved good books, and the books they read had a profound effect on their love for education and their insights into the needs of those around them. The printer in *That Printer of Udell's* and the priest in *Les Miserables* were the kind of strong heroes who helped stimulate their keen intellect and social consciousness. One such idea led to the family's starting a free kindergarten for the mill children of Bonham. This planted a seed that led Charles in later years to start a much needed day-care center in an urban area.

Even when he was a young high school student, the idea of going into the ministry was beginning to take shape in Charles' mind. There were in the area good church camps

and conferences under the guidance of effective directors of Christian education. Another strong influence in Charles' life was the rector of the local Episcopal Church, Richard Morgan. He was Charles' baseball coach and chess instructor. He taught his players about great men, inspired preachers, influential writers, and what it would take to be the best they could be.

Charles was always a baseball fan as well as an ardent player. He broke his leg in one of the games at Bonham High. Nevertheless, he missed playing in only one game in his four years of high school--and that wasn't due to his broken leg. During his senior year, his pastor, Calvin Percy Owen, suggested that if he was going to be a candidate for the ministry he should ask Paris Presbytery to receive him under its care. Presbytery met in Greenville, Texas, on the day his baseball team was scheduled to play.

The Kraemers were eager for Charles to get an excellent education, so there were frequent discussions within the family of his going north to college. Their friend and pastor, Calvin Owen, had graduated from Davidson College in North Carolina. Because of Owen's fine education, Davidson sounded like a good choice for Charles too. He went to Davidson not realizing that many of the people he would meet there were to become friends and colleagues for life.

One of these friends was his roommate Jack Ramseur, who walked with Charles from Davidson College to the nearby town of Cornelius where Charles was to preach his first sermon. On the walk back to school, Charles probed Jack for his opinion of the sermon. The response was one that only a friend would give: "The sermon was okay, but I was a little shocked to see your pants were unzipped."

Charles' preaching in the early years showed signs of his sincerity and wonderful dry wit. He was always prone to preach short and effective sermons in his East Texas way. Whenever possible, he added "off the cuff" remarks that drew his listeners' attention. Even in his early years, his character, his counsel, his speeches, and his letters were those of a special person.

At the beginning of his senior year at Davidson, Charles received a letter from his father telling him about a beautiful new teacher who had come to Bonham. This was the first time he had heard of Beryl Birdsong from Greenville, Texas. Although both of them had finished high school in the class of 1927, she had finished in Greenville and he, in Bonham. The schools were in different interscholastic districts, so they had no occasion to meet. Beryl had gone on to East Texas State for the two years necessary to complete a teacher's certificate and had started teaching before she was twenty. When she went to Bonham to teach, she met Fred and Harriet Kraemer. They ate together in a popular boarding house and became fast friends. The elder Kraemers were charmed by the woman who would become their son's wife.

Beryl, however, was to know Charles' parents for only a short while. In the fall of 1930, only a month after she met his father, Fred was tragically killed in a railroad accident. For two days Charles rode the train from North Carolina to be with his family. The long and tedious train trip was a sad and lonely time for him. To add to his grief and heavy heart, he discovered that his mother had cancer. Harriet Kraemer made it to Charles' graduation in the spring but died in August, a few months later.

Charles met Beryl for the first time not long after his father's death, when he returned home for the Christmas

holidays. All he knew about her was what he had heard from his father. But he was soon to learn why she had been voted class favorite and class beauty at East Texas State.

Charles was quite dismayed to discover that Beryl was "seeing" someone else. It did not take much detective work to find out that the other suitor was the young new physician in town. Charles promptly sent Beryl a large basket of apples with a note saying, "An apple a day keeps the doctor away!"

Having graduated from Davidson with honors, Charles enrolled at Louisville Seminary. During the summer following his first year, he supplied a pulpit in the Troup-Arp-Overton Parish in East Texas. It was 1931 and the depression was beginning to have its impact throughout the land. His lifelong friend Bill Caldwell had dropped out of college because of the depression and was back in Bonham that summer. Since Troup was one of the toughest oil boom towns in Texas, Charles was nervous about going there as an inexperienced pastor and preacher. He asked Bill to go along. When asked why Bill was there, Charles replied that Bill would stay until he found a one-armed deacon to take his place. Both of them boarded with an elder and his wife and had a very interesting summer. At that time, the rangers used the church yard for a jail on Saturday nights.

Bill tells of one trip back to Bonham in Charles' car. He reports, "...I was driving and he (Charles) was sitting in the rumble seat, with his shirt off, getting some sun, and his blond hair blowing in the breeze. We ran across a young fellow who was hitchhiking to Greenville. He kept looking at Charles and at me, and finally asked what we did. I told him my friend was a Presbyterian preacher, and

I was a lawyer (I was studying law). He thought we were weird, apparently, and said he would get off at the next road intersection, which he did."

Charles started dating Beryl that summer. They were married at 10 o'clock on the morning of September 9, 1932, in Beryl's home church in Greenville. The next two years at Louisville were busy years for Charles and Beryl. He served three churches the entire time he was in seminary, and he also took clinical pastoral training. They paid $3 a week for their boarding house and stay and Beryl said it was worth every penny of it (even if the food was lousy!).

Charles received his Master of Sacred Theology degree from Andover-Newton Seminary. More clinical training took him to Boston to Harvard Episcopal Theological School, Massachusetts General Hospital, Boston Psychopathic Hospital, and later, Illinois State Hospital. Throughout his life his numerous speeches reflected his philosophy that one's inner life affects every aspect of the spiritual and intellectual self and has a great bearing on all major decisions of life.

Charles' sister Ann lived with an aunt until she finished high school. Then she lived with Charles and Beryl while she went to college. She moved out when she got married. The Kraemers served a three-church parish in Kentucky: Hawesville, Lewisport, and Morrison. It was there that their first child, Fred, was born in February of 1935. Not long after that they moved to the industrial suburb of North Kansas City, Missouri.

Charles accumulated much experience from clinical training, the rural churches, and the industrial section of Missouri. Best of all, he saw religion as a natural part of life.

One Christmas in Kansas City, the session of the small church found that it had a surplus of funds for the first time in its history. Session members struggled with what should be done with the extra money. Finally they decided to give the money to their young pastor and his family. When they did, Charles took it to a person who needed surgery but could not afford it. It was not long before the session found out about his gift and were not at all surprised. They knew of his concern for people. That was not, however, what they had intended. Determined to help their pastor and his family, they collected, among themselves, a love gift. This time, however, they gave it to a grateful Beryl with instructions to use it on her growing family. About this time their second child, Harriet Jane Kraemer, was born.

A few years later, Charles and Beryl returned to Kansas City for a celebration and stayed in the home of a friend. Charles went to take a shower and soon returned wearing his raincoat. Someone asked, "Charles, why are you wearing a raincoat?" He responded, "What else do you wear when you are in a shower?" Then he admitted that he had forgotten his bathrobe.

The Kraemers left North Kansas City in February 1941 to accept a call from the First Presbyterian Church in Leland, Mississippi. This small town in the Delta was as unique as its people. The Kraemers were there when World War II began. Charles soon volunteered to go as a chaplain, but he was not accepted. This worried him. He wanted to help out in the war, but he redirected his energies instead to serving the church during those trying times. He had almost forgotten that his application for the chaplaincy was on file when notice came that he was to report for service in ten days. There was much scurrying

about as a result of this unexpected summons. It was arranged that all the family furniture would be stored in an attic for the duration of his service. Charles resigned the pulpit. Beryl took the children to stay with her mother in Texas. By now their third child, Phil, had come. Charles became a Navy chaplain.

His old friend Bill Caldwell, who by now had finished law school and had become an F.B.I. special agent, asked Charles why he chose the Navy. Charles responded that his decision was a practical one. Since the trousers were blue and the shoes were black, he would be able to wear them when he got out of the service.

Nine months later he was discharged. By then the congregation in Leland had elected a pulpit nominating committee, so Charles telephoned the chairman and said, "If you haven't found a new preacher, I'm available!" Much to the amusement and joy of the chairman, the committee, the congregation, and the community, Charles and his family returned to Leland. The reaction of a local Baptist was widely quoted: "The Presbyterians must be in a hell-of-a-fix when the Navy decided the congregation needed Charles more than the Navy!"

Early one Sunday morning, an elder called Charles and told him he was sorry that he would not be at worship because he was going bird hunting. Charles' quick response was, "Any bird that would keep you from worship should be shot!"

A church member and friend, Buff Love, suffered from severe food allergies which often resulted in her hospitalization. Charles' family reported that while they were in Leland every time he heard an ambulance he remarked, "I wonder what Buff has eaten now."

During their vacations, Charles and Paul Tudor Jones of the Presbyterian Church of Greenville, Mississippi, agreed to exchange pulpits with one another at an early service, then to preach at their own churches at 11 o'clock. A pulpit committee wanting to hear both men came to the early service in Greenville one Sunday, arriving just in time to hear Charles preach. They then rushed to Leland expecting to hear Paul at the 11 o'clock service. Imagine their surprise, and Charles', when they heard him for the second time that morning!

One Sunday when Phil Kraemer was just beginning to walk, the Leland congregation was delighted to see him follow his father down the aisle. He walked with his hands behind his back and mimicked Charles' flat-footed stride.

During this period Charles visited New York City with his friend Bill Caldwell. As they walked around the city they came upon a sign advertising a burlesque show. Since they were from a small town and had never seen a burlesque show, they decided to go in. It was so crowded that afternoon they had to sit on the very back row. As people left, they moved closer to the front. Bill asked Charles what his parishioners would think of his attending a burlesque show. Charles said that because he preached about sin, he had to know what he was preaching against.

THE CHARLOTTE YEARS

In early 1945, Charles' ministry took him to the First Presbyterian Church in Charlotte. This stately old uptown church, which occupied a full city block in the heart of Charlotte, had been led for more than a quarter of a century by a minister who rather frequently recounted the battles of the Civil War. He had been followed by a minister whose stay was short, so Charles faced an aging congregation filled with strong-willed Scotch-Irish folk with little sense of ministry or mission. Charles' German heritage was to stand him in good stead as he dug in his heels for the bruising battles to come.

Once the imminent move to Charlotte was announced, Charles said, remembering it some years later, "I got as many letters of sympathy as of congratulations from my friends." He then added, "We loved Charlotte." And indeed he did, for he returned to that city for the final years of his life.

His first session meeting was an indication of what lay ahead. He suggested that the elders engage in a program of lay visitation, but they greeted the suggestion with no enthusiasm. He then gently reminded them that this was one of the duties assigned to them in the *Book of Church Order*. Thereupon ensued a lengthy discussion of the question of officers doing things out of a sense of duty versus will. Charles tried to help them see matters in terms of will and opportunity and not in terms of onerous duty. Indeed, he tried to play down the theme of duty altogether. In this process he learned something about the cultural context of these session members when one of them unex-

pectedly said, "Mr. Moderator, there is nothing wrong with duty. Robert E. Lee said that duty was the most sublime word in the English language." Charles was certainly not prepared for an appeal to this particular authority during a session meeting. An elder who had been against the suggestion for lay visitation hastened to say, "Well, if Robert E. Lee said it, it must be correct." Immediately the session unanimously adopted the suggestion, though hardly out of the sense of corporate pastoral care Charles was seeking.

Another of Charles' legacies when he arrived in Charlotte was a Sunday evening service. As he reported some years later, "No one came but Beryl and me--and we didn't want to come. I said, 'Let's not have it anymore.' Someone asked, 'What will session say?' I said, 'Let's not tell them.' It was six months before an elder noticed that we weren't having Sunday evening worship."

One Sunday morning, Charles arrived early for a particular longtime church school class to find all the chairs facing north. He recalled, "We had to get busy and change them back to facing south. They had not faced north since the Civil War and that was enough to start a new denomination."

Early in his ministry in Charlotte he did a unique thing that had a lasting import on the congregation. To everyone on the church roll he mailed a postcard suggesting that it might be a good idea to close the church and indicating that he was going to preach on that very topic the following Sunday. The sanctuary had never been so full. When he mounted the steps to preach that morning, his wonderfully crafted sermon made it plain that he did not like the idea of closing the doors in the vital situation in which the congregation found itself, but unless they faced where they

were and what they could do, the doors might as well be closed. It was the beginning of the change of direction for the congregation and for the city of Charlotte. The vital inner city ministries and outreach programs of the congregation grew from that day. One of the first was the Child Development Center--uptown Charlotte's first day-care center for the children of working parents.

The battles continued. In fact, Dr. Warner Hall, then pastor of Charlotte's Covenant Presbyterian Church, reports, "Sometimes Charles got clobbered. One Monday he walked under the door of what I laughingly called my study. He really was lower than a gnat's ankle." Charles reported that a group of young couples, drawn by his ministry, had joined First Church. Instead of rejoicing, a leading elder rose to protest that he did not know either these young people or their parents and ended by saying, "We just can't afford a lot of miscellaneous people!"

Warner Hall goes on to say, "In those days a motion to buy a new lawnmower by some strange miracle precipitated a two-hour debate on and denouncement of the National Council of Churches."

Some of the sympathy expressed initially to Charles was elicited not only by First Church, but also by Mecklenburg Presbytery. It was often a bitterly divided court of the church. Some people went to the presbytery meetings just to watch the fireworks. On one occasion, the presbytery became so acrimonious and the moderator so confused that, when a standing vote on an issue was called, the moderator could not decide how to tabulate the required vote. At this point, Charles stood and asked for the floor as a matter of personal privilege. He said he thought he could help the moderator. He suggested that the moderator have the entire presbytery stand, then after they all stood, he could tell

half to sit down. From that he would know what constituted a majority of the presbytery. There was a hushed silence in the presbytery as the body took in his proposal. Then the ridiculousness of it all hit them, and there was raucous laughter which broke the tension and allowed the moderator to get control of himself and the situation.

On yet another occasion Charles asked for the privilege of the floor in the middle of a long and boring (and to him meaningless) debate and set everyone at presbytery into shock. He stood and calmly said, "L.S.M.F.T." Thinking he was alluding to the familiar advertising slogan for Lucky Strike cigarettes ("L.S./M.F.T.: Lucky Strike Means Fine Tobacco"), the members of presbytery were confused. Then Charles added, "Let's stand. My fanny's tired." Once again he had broken the tedium of a dull debate to everyone's joy.

It was on the floor of the presbytery that he delivered his most often quoted witticism. The body was having a long and angry debate about the ordination of women to the office of elder. Charles firmly believed in the equality of the sexes and had long fought for women's ordination. When he was granted the floor, in his dry way he said, "Mr. Moderator, we have to be careful about ordaining women. If we let them get a foot in the door, the next thing you know they will be wanting to intermarry with us."

While he was in Charlotte his alma mater, Davidson College, decided to honor him with the Doctor of Divinity degree. The citation written for that occasion read, in part, "Charles Edgar Stanberry Kraemer, inspiring preacher, understanding counselor of troubled minds; recognized leader in your city and in your Synod; Davidson College

is happy to confer upon you the honorary degree of Doctor of Divinity."

Not only was Charles' good friend Warner Hall in Charlotte, but also his friend Jas. A. Jones, who was pastor of Myers Park Presbyterian Church. The three men delighted in playing practical jokes on one another. One Saturday, Charles noticed on the religious pages of the *Charlotte Observer* a small announcement stating that Warner Hall would be Sunday morning speaker at the Baraca Bible Class at a nearby church. Many men's Sunday School classes were named Baraca in the 20s, 30s, and 40s. The headline read: "Warner Hall to be Baraca Speaker." In a day or so, Warner received the following letter: "Dear Dr. Hall, I read with interest in last Saturday's *Observer* that you speak Baraca. I have always wanted to be a speaker of Baraca and would very much like to learn how to do so. I would appreciate it...if you would consent to taking me as a pupil. Sincerely, Charles E. S. Kraemer."

When Charles preached he wore his Geneva gown and added his academic hood on Christmas and other "high days." Such "informality" was a shock to the First Church congregation, who were accustomed to seeing morning coats on the ushers and pastors at all worship services.

His name, of course, always aroused interest. By now his best friends were calling him "Old Three Letters." At the first picnic on the grounds after World War II, someone called out to the new preacher, "Hey, Mr. Kraemer, what does C.E.S. stand for?" Instantly and without pausing in what he was doing, Charles sang out, "Courage, Energy, and Speed."

A live Christmas pageant on the lawn was one innovation that Charles brought to the uptown church. One night he was responsible for getting the sheep from the old

manse garage to their proper place in the pageant. The sheep would have run all over the city had it not been for the iron picket fence that surrounded the church property. He had a great deal of trouble rounding them up. When they were finally in place, he was heard to mutter, "Whoever said that sheep were mild!"

Regarding the pageant, he once confessed, "If we didn't have enough children, we borrowed some Baptists. One night it was cold and we had fires for them to keep warm. One of the shepherds caught his bathrobe on fire and fortunately the fire was put out and he wasn't hurt. But it caused a little excitement. If we'd known that--we'd have gotten a bigger crowd. We could have advertised that we were going to burn a Baptist."

Charles' interest in sports continued, particularly his interest in baseball. Somehow he seemed always to manage to get to the world series--no matter where it was being played. He also developed a fondness for tennis that lasted until Parkinson's disease made it impossible for him to move around the court. Sometimes he would play golf in order to be an "appropriate" guest or to have time to engage in meaningful conversations. They are still laughing around the Charlotte Country Club over the time Charles and some of his preacher friends were teeing off for their round of golf. Charles took a mighty swing at the ball but missed it completely. Again he tried, and again the ball sat safely on its tee. After the third try and the third miss, he turned and asked, "Is there a layman around who can express my thoughts for me?"

Once, while preaching a series for his friend Jack Redhead in Greensboro, Charles found himself on the golf course with Jack, who was a superb golfer. Much the same thing happened as Charles vainly tried to slam the

ball down the fairway. Finally he turned to Jack and complained, "This golf course is lower than the one in Charlotte."

His relationship with people was warm and special. No one else could have joked with Mrs. Acton Porcher as Charles did. Mrs. Porcher was a dowager in the life of the city. She favored long black dresses, carried a silver-tipped cane, had a black choker around her neck with a strand of pearls, and wore a broad-brimmed black hat to complete the picture. One day she was coming out of an uptown bank toward her chauffeur-driven car when Charles nearly bumped into her. He did not, however, greet her. So she called out, "Dr. Kraemer, why are you not speaking to me?" "Law, Mrs. Acton," he instantly replied, "I'm sorry. I didn't recognize you without your tin cup." She chuckled about it the rest of her life.

On another occasion Charles was talking to a lady who was worried about the "unattractive" and "undesirable" people who would be eternally in heaven with her. She said that she was not certain she wanted to go to heaven when she died. "Well, if that is the way you feel about it, I don't think you need worry about it," he replied.

Another example of his unique ability to relate to people concerns a college student. The young man thought he wanted to go to seminary and needed to visit with Charles to talk about his decision. The student called and made an appointment. When the day and hour came, the young man walked into Charles' study, they exchanged greetings, and then they sat down opposite one another. Forty-five minutes later not another word had been said. Charles rose and announced their time was up. Although nothing had been said, Charles knew the young man was going to semi-

nary. The young man became a minister and remembered the incident with bemused joy.

After eight fruitful years in Charlotte, the decision was made to move to Richmond. Much had been accomplished during his stay in Charlotte. The membership of the church grew from 991 to 1,166; the Sunday School enrollment went from 431 to 760. The Church's fellowship hall was constructed and the rather drab prayer meeting room was converted into the lovely, worshipful chapel. The child-care center was inaugurated. The old manse was turned into offices, not only for the congregation but also for Mecklenburg Presbytery and for the Synod's director of religious education.

Charles' decision to leave was not warmly received by the congregation. In fact, Mrs. B. S. (Vard) Howell tried to talk him out of his decision. She had been on the commitee that had called him to Charlotte and had worked closely with him. After having exhausted all the reasons she could enumerate for his not going to Richmond, she finally reminded him of his promise to her mother, Mrs. S. B. Alexander, whom everyone called "Two." He had told her that he would bury her. "You tell 'Two' that I'll bury her anytime she wants!" was his response. Because Dr. Lee Stoffel, his successor in Charlotte, was out of the country when she died years later, he did return to bury her.

He did not make it a practice of returning to Charlotte to conduct funerals, feeling strongly that it was better for the incumbent pastor to minister to families in such circumstances. He did, however, return to Charlotte to hold a funeral service on one other occasion. It was for a lady who had been feuding with her sister for years. In fact, no one knew how long it had been since the two had spoken

to one another. Since there was no minister at the church at the time, Charles returned. Shortly before he went into the pulpit to conduct the service, he visited a few minutes with the surviving sister. When he began the service, he became momentarily confused and named the surviving sister rather than the dead one. There was a gasp from the congregation. But nothing could be done and he continued the service. Afterwards the remaining sister told him not to worry. "Since you have already buried me, you won't have to come back again!" Both of them enjoyed retelling that story.

When it was announced that he was leaving Charlotte, the *Observer* spoke of the sense of loss the entire community felt in its lead editorial:

A LOSS TO US IS A GAIN TO THE CHURCH

In the eight years that Dr. Charles E. S. Kraemer has been pastor of the First Presbyterian Church of Charlotte, he has been a vital and influential member of our community--so much so that we have come to depend on him for a great many civic and spiritual jobs that now must be turned over to someone else.

Naturally we regret to see him leave us, even though he believes he can be of greater service in his new work of training lay workers for the church. What noncommissioned officers are to an army, lay workers are to the church, for it is they--the youth directors, directors of religious education, mission workers, Sunday School teachers, kindergarten workers, and others--who train the younger generation to take over when older members pass on, and who keep

the business of the church in order and its work mov-
ing along.

The Presbyterian Church could hardly have found
a man better qualified to train these noncommissioned
officers, for he has laid heavy stress on them in his
own church here in Charlotte. The results are evi-
dent to anyone who is familiar with the progress and
esprit de corps of the First Church under his pastor-
ate.

We congratulate the General Assembly on its
choice, and our best wishes go with Dr. Kraemer in
his new work. At the same time we can't help feeling
that there is going to be a big vacant spot in the civic
and spiritual life of Charlotte for some time until
pinch hitters can be found to take up where he left
off.

Citizens of his caliber don't come along every day.

At about the same time, his friend Jas. A. Jones was
called to move to Richmond as president of Union Theological Seminary in Virginia. Their colleagues decided to
have a party for both of them at the Myers Park Country
Club. The preachers' party was held in the center section
of the club, while cocktail parties were in progress on
either side. It is no surprise that those at the neighboring
cocktail parties soon complained about the noise, what with
Jas. A., Warner Hall, and Charles throwing lines back and
forth the entire evening. Because he was not moving,
Warner was the M.C. for the occasion. Charles' parting
shot was at him. "Finally, I want to leave you with a
passage I have been thinking about. It's from the story
there in Genesis of Abraham and Isaac, where the old man

turns to those who are with him and says, 'The boy and I go yonder to worship. Tarry ye here with the ass.'"

The congregation also had a party for Charles and his family before they left Charlotte. Unfortunately, he did not make it. Much to his embarrassment and to some other peoples' delight, he developed a case of the mumps. The church party went on and Beryl was the bearer of a message from Charles in the form of a poem. It will not be admitted to the canon of great poems written in English, but it is a typical Kraemer response, poking fun at himself and enjoying getting in his word--even if not in person:

> *My wife wrote a poem which received such acclaim*
> *I now want to try one and share in her fame.*
>
> *Her poem was holy, righteous, and true,*
> *But mine's a confession I want to make to you.*
>
> *I've tried to be humble and stay in my place,*
> *But old Satan has trapped me--I'm puffed up in face.*
>
> *Two meetings I've missed from pathological causes*
> *Since I came to this church, and they've both been my*
>   *losses.*
>
> *First wisdom teeth got me, now mumps has me down,*
> *Ne'er another child preacher you'll want in this town.*
>
> *That the First Church of Charlotte should ever call me*
> *Was one of those things I thought never could be.*
>
> *Said a preacher friend to me, "From the time you arrive*
> *You won't last a year."--another said "Five."*

They thought when you realized just whom you had
    called
You'd all reconsider and I'd be blackballed.

But that one year passed--two, three, and then four
And on beyond that until it's four more.

Eight years that I've been here, and you're nicer now
Than you were when I came, though I hardly see how.

You've prayed with me, worked with me, and taught me
    to know
I won't find better Christians wherever I go.

I won't try to excuse it, for no sin is right,
And this pride may be worst in High Heaven's holy
    night.

But if ever a sin could be thus justified
To have been your pastor is just cause for pride.

Though I had hoped to keep humble, now is my face
    red--
The last thing you'll remember, "He had a swelled
    head."

THE RICHMOND YEARS

On February 1, 1954, Charles became the seventh president of the General Assembly's Training School for Lay Workers in Richmond, Virginia. His expertise in pastoral care, his scholarship, and his knowledge of the church equipped him to be an outstanding president. The years of his presidency saw an unprecedented growth and development of the institution. During his tenure (1954-1974), the academic work rose to graduate status, the number of campus buildings doubled, the endowment more than tripled, and the school became fully accredited.

When Charles moved to Richmond as the new president, he was still recovering from the mumps and was under doctor's orders to remain in bed. Because the president's home was being remodeled, he and his family had to move into rooms formerly used as a women's dormitory. Charles later remembered one of those early days when he was recuperating and still in pajamas: "Everyone was gone and there came a knock on the door. I said, 'Come in.' There was a man from the Virginia Dairies wanting to talk about selling milk to the school. He said, 'I was looking for the president.' And I said, 'I'm the president. We're just planning to take it easy around here.'"

Shortly thereafter, while the Kraemers were still living in the dormitory, Charles was up at 5 a.m. reading his Greek New Testament--as was his custom. Beryl was sound asleep. A gentle knock was heard at the door. Charles opened it to find an anguished seminary student who said he was going to Georgia with a girl from the school. It was time to leave, and she was not there.

Would Dr. Kraemer get her? Obligingly Charles whispered, "Sure." Whereupon Beryl jumped straight up in bed. "Charles Kraemer," she said, "you're not going anywhere in the girls' dormitory at this hour in your pajamas. I'll get her!"

In November of 1954, Charles was inaugurated, and his address on that occasion was inspiring and challenging. A day or so later he received a note from Dr. E. T. Thompson, faculty member at Union Theological Seminary in Virginia, which said, in part: "...(I write) to congratulate you on your magnificent address.... I rejoice in its completeness, the sound philosophy which it represented, the lean muscular prose in which it was couched (not a single word wasted), and the humor which lightened it. It could not have been better."

Charles and Jas. A. Jones, now president of UTS, continued their long-standing friendship, one that frequently manifested itself in clever and humorous incidents. From time to time there was talk of merging PSCE and UTS. Charles opposed this move on humanitarian grounds. "Where on earth could you find Jas. A. a job if we merged?" he asked.

He once introduced Jas. A. to the school's community during the daily chapel service by standing and announcing, "Jas. A. Jones needs no introduction." Then he sat down.

Written communiques from Charles to Jas. A. often crackle with Kraemer's wit:

To Jas. A., May 27, 1960:
Dear James:
I give up. You cannot be reached by telephone. We need to get with you yesterday, or sooner if possible.

To Jas. A., September 30, 1964:
Dear James:
I recall we were talking about having opening exercises together. There was also some thought of having a combined baccalaureate service.
Let me know if you have any ideas on this or anything else, for that matter.

To Jas. A., November 11, 1965:
Dear James:
I'll be glad to talk with you re. this matter before I meet with the deans. That will make the meal cheaper; then you pay for the one where more people are present.

As we have already seen, Charles could make brilliant use of his wit to defuse potentially explosive situations. On one occasion, PSCE was negotiating with architects on the design of a new building (later known as Lingle Hall). Charles wanted the facility to be diverse enough for general use in the theological community of Richmond but at the same time to be designed primarily with the school's needs in mind. Word got out that some folk on the UTS faculty wanted to get involved in the negotiations. This upset Charles, so he called Jas. A.

According to one of the UTS administrators who was present, events unfolded in the following way:

"Mr. Jones, this is President Kraemer. I have an unusual request for you."
"Yes, Charles, what is it?"

"I would like for you to call a meeting of your entire faculty for four o'clock this afternoon."

"Well, that is an unusual request. Are you certain?"

"Yes, I am quite certain!"

"Well, then we will get to it. I trust I will see you there."

"Yes, I will be there."

At four that afternoon Charles marched into the faculty meeting room to find a curious and bemused UTS faculty waiting for him. He carried a long, narrow tube under his arm. To the hastily assembled professors he said,

"I thank you for gathering at my request on such short notice. I know that it has been an inconvenience for some of you. I am most appreciative.

"Now I don't want to take much of your time. As most of you have heard, we are constructing a new building which we have decided to share with you. The building is being built with our General Assembly money. Dr. Jones, if you would help me, I would appreciate it. I want to share with you the facts of this building. Some of you have expressed a great deal of interest, as I understand it, in this General Assembly project."

Then he drew out of the tube some sheets with colored drawings on them. He asked his friend Jas. A. to help him by holding up the series of four drawings. They held up the first one and Charles said, "Now this is one end." That sheet was dropped and a second one held up. "And this is the other end." Then the third sheet, with the comment, "This is one side." Then the fourth and final sheet.

"And this is the other side of our building made possible by the gifts of the church at large." He folded his papers, stuffed them back into the tube, and marched from the room without saying another word. This ploy put an abrupt end to the negative discussion concerning what would become Lingle Hall.

Charles and Jas. A. shared many good times together. One evening, soon after their arrival in Richmond, they attended a baseball game together. A series of meetings had kept them from getting to the game on time, and they arrived to find the home team trailing 3-0. In fact, it was the bottom of the ninth inning and the home team had the bases loaded. Just as the two men walked into the stands, the batter hit a home run. The enthusiastic crowd jumped up and roared its approval. Charles wryly remarked to Jas. A., "Well, what do you know. They've seen us!"

The banter was not restricted to his old Charlotte buddies. When Fred Stair became the president of UTS, the memoranda continued.

To Fred Stair, October 1, 1968:
Sorry to learn of your illness. In the event you do recover, I have some things I want to discuss with you. I will be waiting anxiously and hopefully.

CESK to Fred Stair, April 16, 1969:
(Letter regarding sharing hired faculty)
I would like to talk with you re. arrangements, compensation, etc., at your leisure, which I understand to be most of your time.

Other presidents of theological schools were also beneficiaries of Charles' humor as well as his clear thinking. Al

Winn, former president of Louisville Presbyterian Theological Seminary, recalls,

> We had a little association of presidents of theological schools in the PCUS known as SPATS (Southern Presbyterian Association of Theological Schools). When Mac Richards announced his retirement from Columbia Seminary, I suggested we ought to take some official notice of it: a telegram, flowers, something.
>
> "No cut flowers," said Charles. "We ought to send old Mac a potted plant. He can keep it awhile and send it on to Stitt and when he retires from Austin Seminary, Stitt can keep it awhile and send it on to me when I retire...."
>
> After that, our illustrious organization never took official notice of anybody's retirement.

In the course of another conversation with Charles, Al Winn asked, "What are you going to do when you retire, Charlie?" He replied, "I'm going to put a rocker on my front porch and sit. Then, after two months, I'm going to begin to rock--slowly."

Some time before Mac Richards retired, the members of SPATS (Richards, David Stitt, Frank H. Caldwell, Jas. A. Jones, and Kraemer) were flying from a meeting on a Piedmont DC-3. Their flight took them across the Appalachian mountains, directly into a severe thunderstorm. Lightning flashed around them, the plane's engines sounded unusually noisy and strained, the plane itself was bouncing and lurching, and there was no little anxiety among the passengers. Following a loud crack and a sudden lurch, Charles calmly remarked to his colleagues, "You know,

brothers, if this plane goes down, it'll be a new day for theological education in the Southern Presbyterian Church!"

Charles was instrumental in bringing into dialogue three theological schools located in Richmond and in helping to organize the Richmond Theological Center. Dr. Mike Jones, former Dean of the School of Theology of Virginia Union University, said that Charles' warmth and love of people helped to overcome the administrative nightmares and potential hard feelings which could have arisen among these interdenominational and interracial communities. Jones quipped, "Most of us suffer from 'foot in mouth,' but Kraemer always had 'tongue in cheek.'"

Charles' leadership at PSCE faculty meetings, his chats over coffee in the school "break" room, and his genuine interest in the lives of all the school's employees earned for him the appreciation and affection of faculty and staff alike. He also visited in the faculty members' homes, enjoying while there many memorable conversations.

When Isabel Rogers was seeking a tenured faculty position, she asked Charles to outline the tenure process. She also asked for an explanation of faculty members' rights and privileges once tenure was granted. Charles' response was, "Rogers, if you make it three more years you will be immortal."

For Isabel Rogers, Charles was a man ahead of his time. She recalls that when she was employed by the school women faculty members were paid the same amount as the men--not a principle practiced by the rest of the church colleges and agencies. He brought about such changes quietly, but he was always committed to justice for all people.

Occasionally Charles would play tennis with Isabel Rogers, Lamar Williamson, or Wade Boggs. From time to time they would be joined by persons working with the American Bible Society. With a wave of his hand, Charles would announce to the office staff that he was headed to a meeting of the American Bible Society, take his racquet in hand, and head for the courts.

One day, during the afternoon rush hour, he waited with Lamar to cross the street to the tennis courts. Charles disliked driving on congested streets, and as the heavy traffic taking the commuters from downtown Richmond to their suburban homes passed by, he remarked to Lamar, "There go the peons."

When Charles visited Lamar in his perennially "under construction" home in Montreat, Lamar insisted that he step out onto the temporary boards of a proposed deck--three stories above the ground--in order to see the beautiful view. As Charles did so he dryly inquired, "How many guests have you lost, Lamar?"

Charles always listened carefully to staff members who had concerns. One of PSCE's beloved "institutions" was "Mrs. T."--Mrs. Martin Ryerson Turnbull. Shortly after Charles became president, Mrs. Turnbull, who had lived through years of scrimping and saving and "doing without" as the school's dining room manager, reluctantly made an appointment with him. In her proper Tidewater accent, with her hesitant speech pattern, she began, "Dr. Kraemer, I don't wish to bother you, and I have tried in many ways to avoid having to tell you of this situation, but I believe--I fear--that we are simply going to have to purchase a new refrigerator." Charles' immediate response was, "All right, 'Mrs. T.,' I understand and sympathize. Just go out and buy one immediately." After a shocked silence,

"Mrs. T." replied, "Oh no, Dr. Kraemer, we have to think about it first."

The school's field representative needed to touch base with Charles regarding a college she planned to visit. It was a Monday morning and Charles was nowhere to be found around his office. Someone else was also waiting for an appointment with him. The only information regarding his whereabouts was a cryptic note on his calendar: "WS Committee Meeting." Since no one could interpret the note, the field representative decided to call Beryl. Much to her surprise, Charles answered the phone. "What's going on?" she asked. "We're needing you here at the office." In his slow drawl he replied, "Don't you know what day this is? It's the opening day of the World Series. I'll see you later." And hung up the phone.

James Rawlings Sydnor, then the head of the department of sacred music, had two "musical" encounters with Charles which he vividly recalls:

> My uncle gave a Hammond electronic organ to PSCE as a practice instrument. Since it was located in the practice room next to a number of others, I had the agency add earphones to the instrument so that the organ could generate sound not only through its regular public speakers but, if desired, just to the player through his or her earphones. When I was demonstrating this new gadget to Charles, he said, "I would like to hear an organ recital with the player using his earphones."

> Charles once said that he knew why the walls of Jericho fell down. He said that the children of Israel marched around the walls three days and on the third

day they all played saxophones. The people of Jer-
icho couldn't stand it, so they pushed the walls out
on them.

Charles was noted for rising early in the morning. This
routine did not go unnoticed by his close friend, next door
neighbor, and dean of the faculty, Malcolm McIver. Accustomed to sleeping a little bit later than usual on Saturday mornings, Malcolm became frustrated when Charles
would begin mowing his lawn at 6 a.m. Since he knew
that Charles' behavior patterns were difficult to alter, he
complained to Beryl. He was delighted when she would
not allow Charles to cut the grass before 9 a.m.

However, Charles did continue to bedevil Malcolm by
going to his office at 5 a.m. and writing notes--often to
Malcolm. Charles would always indicate the time the note
was written, just to keep the dean humble.

Charles also liked to tease Malcolm about his efficiency
and administrative abilities. On one occasion Charles met
with some new students immediately after they had had an
orientation with Dean McIver. Having been properly introduced, Charles began his remarks by saying, "Students,
regardless of what Dr. McIver told you, I want you to
know that I am the president here."

In the fall of 1968, the social event to mark the beginning of the school year was a dinner at Camp Hanover.
Both Charles and Malcolm had been on trips to "foreign
lands" recently, and both had been asked to share slides of
their travels with the audience. Each had a projector and
a carousel full of slides. They took turns--first a Kraemer
slide and then a McIver slide. All of Mac's slides were of
buildings and landscapes. All of Charles' slides were of
women, particularly airline stewardesses. Charles observed

that he had established his picture-taking priority before he set out on his trip and that obviously McIver had only snapped shots at random.

Charles never did cotton to graduation ceremonies. He thought of them as merely a time for dressing up, wearing a gown, and having something go wrong. Many times, he complained, the diplomas were not in the proper order and students were given someone else's diploma, to the embarrassment of everyone involved.

During one graduation exercise, with the audience following the printed order of service, Charles overlooked one of the hymns and announced the next order of business. When he finished his announcement he noticed that Dean McIver was making gestures, pointing to his program, and looking quite stricken. Charles looked at his program, then at the audience, and said, "I think Dr. Mac wants us to sing."

Students loved his perceptiveness and sense of humor. Sometimes they themselves were the target of his wit. Sometimes they were struck by the inherent poignancy of many of his humorous comparisons. During the late 50s the television commercials for Marlboro cigarettes featured Julie London's singing "You get a lot to like in Marlboro--filter, flavor, flip-top box." Her song was addressed to a handsome, rugged man of the West who, when he lit his Marlboro cigarette, found himself in "Marlboro country"--the beautiful, clear Western plains. From this Charles derived the following sermon illustration: "If Esau had the benefits of modern advertising, he would have been the Marlboro man."

Those students with no prior knowledge of Charles' wit and informality were often quite surprised by his manner. A prospective student, touring the campus with a guide,

saw Charles as he was leaving his office. He wore a sweatshirt given to him by the faculty which had "COACH" on it. As soon as he walked by, the prospective student said, "Oh, there went the coach. I didn't know PSCE had a team."

Once a student went to see the president in his office. When he entered, Charles was sitting behind a small table. Puzzled, the student asked why he did not have a large desk and a big chair like most presidents of institutions. Charles told him, "If you have a big desk, people put a lot of things on it and that means that you do a whole lot of work. I've got a little table so they put little things on it and I don't have as much work to do!"

Students enjoyed teasing Charles. Although they treated him with respect, they would find ways to outwit him when they could. Once, during a Christianity and Human Development class, he was explaining the psychology of guilt and told the story of a young girl who had been reared in a very strict family. Soon after she had been admonished by her mother about the evils and the sin of kissing, she found herself with a young man who was particularly attractive to her. She went with him behind the barn where they shared a kiss. Because she had been taught that this was wrong, she was filled with guilt and developed the habit of regularly biting her lips for their misbehavior. She would bite them so much they were often bloody. Charles used this story to explain the physical as well as the psychological scars which guilt can cause.

At the end of the story, it was time for a break. As was his custom, Charles went to his office to check for messages. When he returned to the classroom, the students were in their seats, each one chewing on his or her lips. Both

teacher and students enjoyed the practical joke, and his illustration was firmly lodged in their minds.

On another occasion Charles announced to his students that he was going to West Virginia and would miss the following week's class. Since class would not be meeting, he was giving them an extra reading assignment which they would discuss following his return. One student then asked, "If the plane crashes while you're on your trip, will we still have class on Friday?"

Charles said that he would let the class know. Two days later a postcard from West Virginia appeared on the school bulletin board: "I made it. Class as usual. Charles E. S. Kraemer."

Not only was Charles an outstanding scholar, but he also enjoyed being creative in his teaching. Once, when he was team-teaching with Sara Little, they decided to role play the Pharisees and the Sadducees. Sara recalls that Charles played the "Chief Pharisee" with relish.

During one Christmas season, Charles and Beryl were in the Miller and Rhoads department store in downtown Richmond. There they encountered a student and her husband. After they had exchanged pleasantries, she asked if they were having any luck shopping. Charles looked bemused and said, "We just had a bad experience. Beryl asked the clerk if they had any invisible wire, and the clerk said that they did not. I asked her, 'How do you know?' She didn't answer."

Another student recounted a talk he had with Charles when he was considering a position in a church in Kansas City, Missouri. The student knew that Charles had once served a church there and would be familiar with the area. Once the discussion got to the climate and weather conditions, Charles said, "You must realize that Kansas City is

on the plains in the middle of the United States, and it can feel like it is 115 degrees in the summer time."

"Well, I understand that," the student responded, "but being from South Carolina, I imagine I can get used to hot summers. I also imagine that in the winter it would be fairly mild."

Charles was incredulous. "Mild winters? No way! There is nothing between Kansas City and the North Pole but a barbed wire fence!"

Kansas City was the destination of one of Charles' more interesting flights to speak at a presbytery event. On the evening of his expected arrival, a PSCE graduate and Charles' sister (who lived in Kansas City) drove to the airport to meet him. It was a stormy night. A strong wind had been blowing and the rain was coming down in sheets. All the passengers leaving the airplanes looked sick. Finally Charles' plane landed. When the door opened, its passengers emerged looking even worse than those coming from other airplanes. Many, in fact, were still nauseated. Finally, Charles came through the door, looking fit and healthy. As she greeted him his sister observed, "Charlie, it looks like you had a horrible flight!"

Charles said, "It was just terrible! Half the people were sick. At one point I looked out the window, and the plane was shaking heavily and the wings were flapping up and down like a buzzard's."

"My heavens, Charlie," she said, "weren't you worried to death?"

"No, I didn't care. It's not my airplane," he replied.

On another occasion, Charles announced to his class that he would need a ride home from the airport following an upcoming trip. As an incentive, he promised to buy an ice cream cone for the student who met him. When his plane

landed, several carloads of students were waiting on the runway, complete with flash bulbs, paper leis, and "Welcome home, Mr. President" signs. He took these gifts, along with the astonished bewilderment of his fellow passengers, as his due, nodding and smiling graciously at the crowd. On the way home he bought every student an ice cream cone.

Charles was surprised when he arrived one day to lead chapel to find the room full of ladders and painters. But his verbal facility and his adaptability rescued him. "You may wonder," he began, "why these ladders and painters are here. I arranged to have them as a liturgical device to point your thoughts to heaven."

One of the buildings constructed on the campus during Charles' presidency was a dormitory. The space was desperately needed. After the first year of construction only the first two floors were completed. The third floor was being built above the students as they enjoyed their new quarters beneath. One day, a student encountered Charles as he came down a ladder from the construction area. "You know," he said, "I think we'll just continue building until we get to heaven."

"And call it the Tower of Babel?" the student asked.

"No," he replied, "the house that Charlie built."

The dormitory would later be named "Kraemer Dormitory"--after he left the presidency.

When a student told Charles shortly before she graduated that she would be working at the Independent Presbyterian Church in Birmingham, Alabama, he promptly alerted her to the realities of the church. "I think," he said, "you should know that there is no such thing as an independent Presbyterian church."

During the discussion of a new name for the school, Charles noted the similarity between the initials PSCE and his own (CESK). He enjoyed devising ways to convert the "P" into a "K." He toyed with the possibility of spelling traditional Presbyterian words with a "K"--such as "Kovenant" and "Kalvin." Facetiously he suggested a move to Louisville so that the name of the school would be "Kentucky School of Christian Education." He abandoned that idea, however, because he feared it would make him sound too much like Colonel Sanders.

Throughout Charles' tenure as president, Sara Little's handwriting was considered inscrutable. Charles once encountered a group of students attempting to decipher her comments on their papers. "That's the wonderful thing about Sara," he said. "She lets you figure out for yourselves what is important to notice." The student recalling this incident said, "The more I've thought about this story, the more it has taught me about two great teachers."

Students were required to submit projects, known as "verbatims," in Charles' counseling course. These verbatims were supposed to be records of dialogues between the students and persons experiencing problems and were analyzed in class to determine the students' skills in listening and responding appropriately. As is often the case in academe, several students waited until the last minute to complete the assignment. Attempting to explain to Charles why they were so sleepy the day of the class meeting, they said, "We spent most of last evening riding buses up and down Chamberlayne Avenue, trying to strike up conversations in order to uncover crisis situations."

"You should use that technique on the tennis courts," said Charles. "I win a lot of games that way."

The relationships between the students at UTS and PSCE were perennial topics of discussion, particularly the question of which school was academically sounder. The fact that the schools faced each other across Brook Road led to some good-humored banter between not only their respective student bodies but also the two faculties.

The frequency and number of marriages between the women of PSCE and the men of UTS seemed always to invite comments. So much so that the two institutions came to be known as the "match factory." Charles was quick to explain that the men from the seminary were the sticks and the women from PSCE were the heads.

On occasion Charles and Beryl were not above playing the role of matchmaker. William E. Thompson recollects the following:

> In 1959 I was about to become engaged to an ATS/PSCE alumna who was working in a Richmond church. My wife-to-be had not only been a Kraemer devotee at the school, she had also been his parishioner in Charlotte, and their families were close friends. My parents came to Richmond, ostensibly to visit me but mainly to meet my "special friend." My father had been a college classmate of Dr. Kraemer, and because of that and because Charles and Beryl had been part of the "cupids" in our relationship, the Kraemers had my parents drop by their house for refreshments. Dr. Kraemer was trying to make a point of hearty endorsement to them about my energetic friend. He said, "We had to crank up our children by hand, but this girl obviously has a self-starter."

Months later, when the Kraemers greeted us after our wedding, Charles said, "Folks tell you that marriage is bliss...but first come the blisters."

One of the jobs of a president of an institution of higher education is to meet and socialize with the school's constituents. Charles handled these contacts with flair, and many stories emerge from them. Once he spoke at a supper at Richmond's Second Presbyterian Church. Surveying his place setting at the head table, he said, "I always suspected it, and it's true. This is a two-fork church." The name stuck, and Second Church is still referred to affectionately by some of its members and others as a "two-fork church."

One Sunday he preached at Second Church, and the next morning he could hardly wait to share with a trusted staff member the reaction of a redoubtable dowager to his sermon. She bore down upon him as he stood at the door, seized his hand, and gushed, "Oh, Dr. Kraemer, I am so delighted that you chose to preach on this day about the Meades and the Persians. You see, my mother was a Meade."

He continued to use his sense of humor to defuse potential moments of crisis. He recounted one of those moments:

I was attending a meeting on Christianity and Health in connection with a National Evangelistic committee of the Council of Churches. Seward Hiltner, with whom I had studied in our Clinical Pastoral Education program, was the national leader. I was the local leader in this particular part of the meeting. Seward was leading the group in the consideration of making funerals more Christian. He said, by way of

41

illustration, "For instance, the hymn 'Beautiful Isle of somewhere' is pagan in its theology."

One of the members of the group immediately responded, "When my wife wrote that hymn she did not consider it pagan. Now if you had used the illustration of 'Going Down the Valley One by One' I would agree with you.

There was one of those painful embarrassed silences and something led me to ask, "Is the author of 'Going Down the Valley One by One' here today?" Seward always insisted that it was the Holy Spirit who led me to ask that question at that time.

As people disagreed with his liberal and open attitude about many social issues, Charles frequently became the target for anger and frustration. After one particularly confrontational experience, he said, "Presbyterians don't get angry in church; they just get hurt. The peculiar thing is that when Presbyterians get hurt, they act just like other people act when they get angry."

He chose to become involved in the life of the city of Richmond. He recounts one incident which capitalizes on the city's strong consciousness of its history:

Being in Richmond, those of us who had come from other parts of the country naturally looked to Grace Covenant Presbyterian Church to keep us aware of the facts related to "the WAH" (the Civil War). The church, located on the famous Monument Avenue, was not far from the UDC (United Daughters of the Confederacy) Headquarters building.

One day as we passed the UDC headquarters, I was asked "What are the UDC's?" to which I re-

sponded, "I think it was the WACs from Civil War Days."

Charles' community involvement included regular visits with prisoners on death row at the Virginia State Penitentiary. As a gesture of friendship, one of the prisoners gave him a painting which still hangs in the Kraemer home. He managed to brighten the inmates' days with his humor. One day laughter could be heard throughout the cell block. When Charles entered death row where the "hardened" criminals are held, he announced loudly, "Well, I see all my friends are here today."

On May 18, 1968, the city of Richmond was asked to host the 450 participants in the "Poor People's March on Washington," part of the Civil Rights movement. Coming so soon after the assassination of Dr. Martin Luther King, Jr., it was not only a massive undertaking but also one fraught with tension and uneasiness. The participants in the march were mainly sharecroppers from all over the South. Richmond was scheduled to be the next-to-last stop for the group. They would require food, housing, entertainment, emergency health services, and massive police protection.

Under Charles' leadership hundreds of volunteers from throughout the city met the group's many needs. Much of the activity took place on the PSCE campus since the Richmond Theological Center had agreed to host the group. Charles took on major responsibilities for the affair, well aware there would be negative consequences across the city and in the church at large. In her book *The First Seventy Years, A History of the Presbyterian School of Christian Education*, Louise McComb writes, "His (Charles') decision showed courage, but most importantly, it demonstrat-

ed his own values and his loving concern for all persons--who are made in God's image, and therefore have worth in His sight. His decision and example did not go unnoticed by the students or the community."

In June of 1974, a bittersweet event occurred that marked the end of the Kraemer era at PSCE. It was Alumni/ae Day, always a major event in the life of the institution. This was more important than usual because it was to be Charles' final occasion before he retired. Warner Hall came up from Charlotte to act as Master of Ceremonies, and Glenn Bannerman and his students staged a puppet show that recounted many of the humorous events which had taken place during Charles' tenure. The Alumni/ae Association marked the occasion with a scholarship endowment honoring both Charles and Beryl.

The fun and bright balloons, however, could not conceal the underlying sadness of the event. Charles had served with distinction as president for twenty years. More than that, he had touched countless lives--enriching them with his warm wisdom and kind wit. The school and those who had contact with it during his years would forever be changed. In her book, Louise McComb describes Charles' style of leadership as "relaxed, warm, personal, nonmechanical, low-keyed, humorous." It is no wonder he touched so many lives in that diverse community.

THE YEAR AS MODERATOR

In 1973 Charles served as the 113th Moderator of the Presbyterian Church in the United States. He kept a scrapbook as a record of his year as moderator. On the first page of the book there is a postcard from Balmer Kelly, a friend and professor at UTS, which reads, "A British dictionary has as one definition: Moderator: a mechanical contrivance designed to control the flow of gas. We miss you and Beryl--take care. Balmer." Such is typical of the humor with which Charles remembered the year he held the highest office in his church.

Originally there had been three other candidates for the office of moderator, but by the time the assembly convened, Charles was the only one who actually ran for the office. Having a single candidate for moderator was a rare occurrence for the church. It had happened previously only twice before: in 1950, when Dr. W. Taliaferro (Tolly) Thompson was elected; and in 1956, when Dr. Ben R. Lacy was elected.

It had become the custom to have an open forum with the candidates on the night before the election so that the assembly could get better acquainted with the candidates and their views before voting. This custom was adhered to even though there was only one candidate. Almost the first question asked went something like this: "Dr. Kraemer, we all know that you are a much loved man with many friends all across the church. Would you please tell us who are your best friends and why?"

Those present recall that there was a long pause while Charles collected his thoughts. Then he said, "Well, I

have to say I am my best friend." The commissioners thought this was hilarious and burst into laughter. He looked confused for a moment but then rode over their laughter by saying, "I did not mean for that to be funny. I really am my best friend. It seems to me that is a requirement of the second commandment." He then went on to give a moving and eloquent statement about the need for us to love ourselves so that we can love our neighbors. The commissioners sat in hushed amazement and joy.

The next morning, as voting time drew near, an acquaintance noticed that Charles seemed more nervous than usual. Questioned about this, Charles said he thought it was only natural to be nervous; he did not want to be known as the only candidate who failed to get the necessary majority when there was no opposition.

After the election, when he was being escorted to the platform to receive the gavel and the traditional Celtic cross, he remarked to those around him, "Remember when you see a turtle on a stump that someone has put him there."

As was the case in most church assemblies of the era, this General Assembly faced the controversial issues of abortion, the Watergate scandal, and the war resistance movement. The biggest denominational issue, however, was the movement of a number of conservative congregations to leave the denomination to form the Presbyterian Church in America. It was a tense time for the denomination, the General Assembly, and the moderator, who said he was "ready to spend all the prayer, ready to spend all the time, ready to spend all the patience that could be profitable to bring healing to our church." He also pointed out that the first split in Presbyterianism in the United States occurred less than a quarter of a century after the establish-

ment of the denomination in 1741. He was therefore not overly optimistic about reconciliation.

Even then *The Presbyterian Journal* (now the publication of the PCA) expressed the views of those who did not like the General Assembly nor trust the leadership of the PCUS. Yet in its summary of the 113th General Assembly it had this to say: "The 1973 Assembly was unquestionably the fairest Assembly within recent memory. Every point of view got a fair hearing and frequently the voting reflected the constitutional position of the Church rather than the majority opinion of the commissioners." In its comments on Charles Kraemer it had this to say: "...having been elected by acclamation, he was 'everyone's moderator!' His fairness and wit were catching...."

Examples of his wit abound. When putting one motion before the assembly, Charles asked those favoring the motion to say "aye," which they dutifully did. Then he called on those opposing it to say the same thing. With eyes twinkling, he reported to the assembly, "The ayes have it!" At another time, following the discussion of an item referred to simply as "Paragraph O," Charles asked all those in favor of adopting O to say "O." And they did.

This General Assembly, which was held in Fort Worth, was Stated Clerk James A. Mallard's final one after serving 14 years in that position. Charles confided to the commissioners, "If you see me asking him lots of questions, it's not because I don't know the answers. I want him to feel wanted."

Once, not certain that his microphone was on, he asked the commissioners if they could hear him. "No!" they responded. "Do you want to hear me?" he then asked.

Presiding at the General Assembly is just the initial duty of the moderator. Most of the year is spent on the road--

interpreting the church to members and delivering speeches not only in this country but also in foreign mission fields.

The Kraemers' overseas trip was to Africa, to the Union of South Africa as well as to some of the smaller countries where historically the Presbyterian Church provided strong mission programs. On the continent he spoke to women's groups, church educators, and leadership groups of the indigenous churches. He also carried greetings from the General Assembly to sister bodies on the continent. Before making the overseas trips, he had traveled throughout the Southeastern United States speaking at seminaries and to local churches, attending board meetings and meetings of various presbyteries.

It was, as has been noted, a tense time. Yet in the states of the Deep South he served as a moderating influence in the rising tide of the conservatives' withdrawal movement. His talk on this subject was titled "Who Wants to Be a Presbyterian?" There were, however, certain churches whose sessions refused to allow him to speak.

His records indicate he made over 140 addresses, speeches, or presentations during the year. He traveled over 53,000 miles and spoke to over 31,000 people, not counting the many people who watched him on television.

It is the custom of the church to stand when a moderator first appears at a gathering. During this time Charles was still president of PSCE. The faculty there asked him if he, as moderator, would expect them to stand as he entered a room. He replied that he certainly did! They took great delight in doing so the first time he returned, but, to his relief, after that they returned to their old ways.

THE FINAL YEARS

Charles and Beryl built a house in Davidson, North Carolina, in preparation for his retirement. They moved there with their son Fred in June of 1974. It was a comfortable home, located on a wooded lot not far from the Davidson College campus. The plan was for him to become an adjunct professor of religion at the college, do some writing, and work with the Southern Association of Presbyterian Institutions of Higher Education. Although Charles had jested that he was going to sit on the deck and learn to rock, he was far too restless and creative to do so.

From these days comes a story about a class in religion he was teaching. One of the students happened to be young Ernest Barry, whose family had been close to the Kraemers when they were in Charlotte. During class one morning, Charles asked for questions. There was a pause, and then Ernest raised his hand and asked Charles if he believed that ducks went to heaven. An astonished Charles inquired, "Why do you ask that, Ernest?" "Well," he replied, "when my mother was a child, her pet duck died and you told her when you came and buried it that it had gone to heaven." Charles said, "Ernest, if it was true then, it must be true now!"

Charles soon began to write for the newspaper of the Synod of North Carolina, a project he continued until a few weeks before his death. His contributions were often witty and always provocative, a series of comments on life in general and on the problems and issues that faced the church in particular.

49

The pull of Charlotte and old friends enticed Charles and Beryl back to that city after only two years in Davidson. They bought a small brick house in their old neighborhood and moved back there in June of 1976.

Beryl moved her church membership back to First Presbyterian Church when its outreach committee urged her to do so. Charles became a strong and quiet supporter of the pastor, Carswell Hughes. There were already close ties because Carswell's wife Ina was the daughter of Charles' old friend, Jas. A. Jones. The congregation soon elected Charles as pastor emeritus. This designation he took seriously by unobtrusively visiting the elderly and those in the hospitals. He refused, however, to take part in any baptisms, funerals, or weddings even when urged to do so by Carswell. He knew that former pastors could, and often did, cause problems. And he was determined not to be a problem for either Carswell or Bill Wood, who followed Carswell as pastor of First Church.

At times Charles' determination on this matter posed problems. Once Carswell was expected to attend an important meeting out of town and a funeral had to be conducted. He tried to cajole Charles into substituting for him. "Charles," Carswell pleaded, "I must be out of town. I have no choice. What am I to do? You must help me. Please conduct the funeral." Charles responded, "How shall I explain all that to the family? That you must be out of town and I am substituting? What do you want me to do? Work it into the prayer?" He did not hold the service.

On another occasion, Carswell tried to convince Charles to baptize a baby. There was much discussion between the two men. With his eyes twinkling, Charles finally countered, "Carswell, I just cannot. Fact of the matter is, my

baptisms are so good that if I agree to come, no one would ever ask you to baptize again."

Yet Charles regularly took part in the congregation's ministry to the "street people," the homeless transients in our cities who continually seek help from the uptown churches. Once a week he took his turn at counseling until Parkinson's disease made him too weak and disabled to be of assistance. He enjoyed his contacts with others and the sense of accomplishment this gave him. His work in this ministry also served as an inspiration to the people of the congregation.

In 1982, First Presbyterian Church celebrated its 150th year as an organized congregation. As part of this celebration, there was a well-produced pageant. Those who were present will long remember with special fondness one scene. Ward McKeithen portrayed Charles and used excerpts from the memorable Kraemer sermon "Shall We Move from Uptown Charlotte?" In this sermon Charles had convinced the members they were called to remain in their present location to serve as a people of God in the heart of Charlotte. Just before he left the pulpit, Ward leaned forward and said, "God bless you, Charlie Kraemer!" It was a fitting tribute to Charles and to his wisdom and vision on that special occasion in the life of the congregation.

During the celebration all the living former ministers were invited to attend the worship service on a particular Sunday morning. When Charles was introduced, he said, "I am certainly glad to be counted among the living." The congregation laughed uproariously.

In spite of growing health problems, Charles and Beryl continued their active social life, enjoying a variety of friends and neighbors, going out to eat, exchanging funny

51

stories, and taking part in the life of the church. They also enjoyed keeping up with their children and grandchildren. Fred remained in the home with them. Jane lived in Kingsport and Phil in Norfolk, and there was much traveling back and forth among the three households. When Jane's two children later moved to Charlotte, Charles and Beryl were delighted.

Charles was active in the life of Mecklenburg Presbytery and, for a period of time, had the onerous task of writing the resolutions of thanks which conclude each presbytery meeting. As one would expect, the resolutions written by him were models of brevity and wit. Much to their own amazement, many members of presbytery found themselves staying to the end of the meeting just to hear his resolutions, something they rarely did otherwise. One resolution began,

> *In a world where a microscopic silicon chip can record a billion angels dancing on the head of a pin, where Dr. Patrick Osmer, director of the Inter-American Observatory, has just announced that he has seen the edge of the universe through a 158 inch telescope, a universe which was born 8 billion years ago, or 4000 years ago, in a world where "1000 years in the sight of the Lord is but as yesterday when it is past," Mecklenburg Presbytery met for a long day in its 41st Session....*

In another pithy poke at the presbytery, a portion of the resolution reads,

> *Having enjoyed the hospitality of Covenant Church many times in the past, we could have written our*

appreciation to them before we even got here. We offered a warm round of applause during lunch for those who provided the meals and refreshments. Such an expression to those volunteer helpers has become and probably will continue to be a tradition with us. It is so much less expensive to applaud them than to pay them....

Yet another one began,

The service to the Presbytery began at once with the Plaza members in the parking lot who told us where to go. When there was noise in the rear of the church early in the meeting, the women of the church restored quiet, thus fulfilling the ancient admonition, "Let women keep silence in the church."

This committee report ended with the following words:

We note with appreciation that the Chase Manhattan Bank, on the eve of the Fall Meeting of Mecklenburg Presbytery, lowered the prime interest rate to nineteen-and-one-half percentage and we are grateful to the truly needy members of this community for not coming to this meeting to disturb our comfort. Thanks also to those who stayed long enough to hear this report--both of you!

Charles also remained active in the life of the denomination. Because he was a former moderator, he and Beryl were expected to attend the annual meetings of the General Assembly. In addition, he was pleased to be on the committee that led to the reunion of the Presbyterian Church,

U.S. ("Southern") and the United Presbyterian Church, U.S.A. ("Northern"). Together with his friend Frank Caldwell, Charles wrote the motion that ended the life of the "Southern Church" and led to the formation of the Presbyterian Church (U.S.A.).

Charles also led the fight within the PCUS for the ordination of Christian educators. In that endeavor he was successful, for the last two General Assemblies of the denomination and the requisite number of presbyteries approved the plan of ordination. However, it was one of the last acts of the PCUS and was not included in the articles forming the new denomination. Undiscouraged, Charles and his fellow educators continued the struggle in the new church. There they did not prevail, but Charles won many friends for the cause, and the issue is still very much alive for many people.

When Parkinson's disease began to take its toll, Charles decided to discontinue his work for the Southern Association of Presbyterian Institutions of Higher Education. This organization, consisting of the presidents of colleges related to the PCUS, was not at all pleased with his decision. But the presidents understood and dispatched Bun Perkinson, president of St. Andrew's Presbyterian College, to present their gift to Charles. It was a beautiful pair of antique brass candlesticks. Bun fondly recalls that Charles took them in his hands as though weighing them, turned to Beryl, and said, "Beryl, they seem to be real."

Charles had to undergo heart by-pass surgery. When faced with a heart attack and then heart failure, he asked his doctor, "Isn't your work under warranty?"

While in Richmond Charles had served as interim pastor at the Grace Covenant Presbyterian Church. Once word of his surgery reached the congregation of that church, a letter

was sent to him stating that the session had voted 13-12 to send him a "get well" message. Charles' "thank you" note read, "That's the closest thing to a unanimous vote we'll ever see from that session."

After one particularly serious encounter with the surgeon's knife, Charles' recovery did not seem a sure thing and everyone was worried about his health. Then one day, in a very weak whisper, he told Beryl to ask his lawyer to come to see him. She did so at once, thinking that perhaps he might want to change his will or tend to other legal matters. When the lawyer arrived, Charles haltingly said he did not have any real business for the lawyer but asked him please to stand at the head of his bed on the right side for a while. The lawyer and Beryl thought it a peculiar request and wondered if he was delirious. Before too long, Charles asked Beryl to call for the doctor and insisted that the lawyer stay where he was. The doctor came in, and Charles assured him he did not need to have his pulse taken, that he was satisfied with his treatment, but would the doctor please stand at the head of his bed on the left side, opposite the lawyer. By now everyone was thoroughly puzzled and quite concerned. For a few minutes they stood there in silence with Beryl looking on. Finally she could stand it no longer and asked, "Charles, what in the world is going on?" In the strongest voice they had heard in quite sometime, he replied, "I just wanted to die like my Savior did--between two thieves!" They knew then that they no longer had to worry about him. His humor was back. He was well on his way to recovery.

Soon after the operation Charles and Beryl journeyed to Montreat. When he entered the lobby of the Assembly Inn, he found an American Red Cross blood donation unit set up. The faces of the Red Cross volunteers must have

registered real amazement when Charles, wearing Bermuda shorts that plainly revealed the extensive scars on his legs from his recent heart surgery, announced, "I'd like to make a withdrawal, please."

Later, he was asked to speak to a group of college presidents meeting on the campus of Southwestern at Memphis (now Rhodes College). During his speech, Charles explained that some might have a difficult time understanding him as his medicine made his mouth dry. "Don't worry, Charles," responded Jim Daughdrill, the young president of Southwestern, "I always thought you were too dry anyway." Without hesitation Charles fired back, "I'd rather be dry than always wet behind the ears, Jim."

Charles was not the only one who had health problems. His old friend Warner Hall also had Parkinson's disease. For these proud men, it was a horribly debilitating disease. As it progresses, one slowly becomes weaker and weaker and gradually less able to care for oneself. Yet the two men were determined to remain independent as long as they could--and, of course, to continue their long-standing friendship. It was a sad but common sight to see the two of them shuffling along the sidewalks of Charlotte taking their daily walk together. Once someone stopped to chat and asked if they were engaging in a lively and entertaining theological discussion as they walked. No, this was not the case, Charles said. They were just trying to stay on the sidewalk and were encouraging each other to keep moving.

As long as he could, Warner worked for Davidson College. His office was in a church near one of the city's leading nursing homes. The two decided they had better not take their daily walks past the home lest someone conclude they were runaways.

John Kuykendall, the president of Davidson College, reports an encounter with Charles as he was shuffling into the annual barbecue the Harry and Bryant Funeral Home held for Charlotte's ministers. Chuckling, Charles said, "Do you know what my son Fred told me when I said I was coming over to the funeral home for lunch? He said, 'Keep moving!'"

A few seconds later, as the two continued toward the lunch, a cat jumped out of the shrubbery and ran across the street. Charles quipped, "There goes one that escaped the barbecue."

Charles and Beryl visited Richmond and PSCE one last time. He delivered the Founders' Day address and captivated another generation of students with his clear use of scripture, his wise words of encouragement, and his sly humor. He began by observing, "Whenever people of my age group, or to use the language of education, whenever people in my developmental stage receive an invitation to speak, the first thing we do is to accept. I have heard that is especially true of old preachers. After we have accepted an invitation to speak there is time enough for such details as whether we have anything to say, whether our voice will be able to meet the challenge, and how much we can trust our memories. Mark Twain said that when he was younger he could remember everything that happened, whether it had happened or not...." From there he went on to sketch the purpose of the school, his hope for the ordination of educators, and the real need in the church for trained leaders.

The Kraemers took one other major journey together. It was to Fort Worth for the annual meeting of the Association of Presbyterian Educators. Charles had always been a favorite of the group, and they had decided to honor him

with a special membership plaque. They asked that he and Beryl make the special effort to come to Fort Worth and that he address the group. Charles began his address--his speech was slurred now--by saying he hoped the group would put up with his disability. He wanted it clearly understood "that I've got age--that is A G E, not aids--A I D S. They sound a lot alike."

Naturally, the slow decline was both humiliating and discouraging for Charles. He did not want to be a burden nor did he want to be in an institution. He had seen his friend Warner Hall moved first to a hospital and then to Sharon Towers, the Presbyterian retirement home in Charlotte. Charles continued to visit Warner there at least weekly until he found it impossible to get in and out of a car.

Perhaps the thing he missed most was going out with friends to Mexican restaurants. He loved hot foods. In fact, at one point he claimed to have cured his ulcer with Texas Pete and Coca Cola. He would often amaze waiters and waitresses by asking them to take the dishes back--sometimes their spiciest, hottest items--to be made spicier and hotter. One of his final meals out was with a small group of close friends. During the meal, one of them noticed that he kept wiping his mouth. When he saw the look of concern, he said, "Oh, don't worry about it. Every time Beryl looks at me I wipe my mouth."

Despite the steady decline and the frequent discouragement, he continued to find humor in his situation and readily agreed with his good friend Vard Howell and others who declared that "Old age is not for sissies."

Two of Charles' last articles in the Synod of North Carolina's newspapers were quite different in mood from his previous articles. One reflected the feeling of uselessness

and purposelessness of the old. The other stressed the importance of being with God's people in worship and included a quiet tribute to his lovely and courageous companion Beryl.

She found an electric bed for him and, for the last week, a wheel chair. She continued to help him get dressed and do the other things that made him feel whole. She encouraged people to visit and to engage in lively conversations in his presence. He could hardly take part, but now and again he would raise his hand. Someone would notice and say that Charles wanted to say something. All conversation would cease as everyone listened intently to what he had to say. Usually those gathered around him could figure out what he was saying and would be delighted by his contribution.

On the Saturday before he died, Fred and Junie Stair came to call. The Stairs were longtime friends from the Richmond days. Charles and Junie loved to share stories. She told one that really struck his funny bone, and laughter racked his feeble frame. Before anyone quite knew what was happening, his fingers were racing across the typewriter keyboard as he typed out one of his favorite stories with eyes dancing. Junie laughed so hard that Fred became concerned about her bronchitis and took her home.

One day Charles had fallen going up the three steps to his front porch. He completely disappeared in the bushes beside the steps. Beryl could not find him. He later reported he thought he was going to die there. She said she could not imagine what had happened to him; one minute he was behind her and the next he was nowhere to be seen. She did not hear a thing. They decided that Charles would wear a whistle so he could always call for help, even if his

voice was gone. He was wearing the whistle when he died.

EPILOGUE

By Tuesday, June 21, 1988, Charles had grown so weak that he finally asked to be taken to the hospital. Two days later, on Thursday the 23rd of June, he died of heart failure. His beloved Beryl and two other members of the family were present.

Bill Wood and Jane Fobel conducted a memorial service for him in Charlotte's stately old First Church, the uptown church he had inspired to stay put and keep moving. Bill Wood reminded the congregation that Charles did not want it said of him when he died, "Oh, but isn't it a blessing that he is gone!" Those who knew him and loved him simply could not conceive of his absence from their lives as a blessing.

There were memorial services as well in Richmond, at PSCE, and in Montreat, at the annual Christian Education Conference.

The heart of the service in Richmond was called "Moments of Memory." All who wished to do so shared their expressions of gratitude to God for the life of Charles Kraemer. One by one, people stood and recalled memorable moments in which their lives had been touched by his in a variety of contexts: at a civic club meeting, on the board of trustees of a charitable organization, in jail, at church, on a summer cruise, in his office, the chapel, a classroom or a tennis court at the Presbyterian School of Christian Education. Like musical motifs, the same themes linked these remarks: Charles' pastoral sensitivity, his practical justice, his incomparable wit, and his common sense, together with a rich mixture of joy, grief, and love

that spilled over in those who had been warmed and blessed by his friendship. All kinds of people, all sorts of situations; one inimitable Charles Kraemer.

Lamar Williamson led a litany of thanksgiving for Charles' life and the gifts God gave him:

For the warmth and breadth of his spirit: his love for all sorts of people; his sensitivity and accessibility to those in trouble; his disarming humor in the face of tension and hostility; his lighthearted simplicity and deep integrity; his unassuming courage and tenacious faith;
    We give you thanks, O God.

Some years ago, James T. Cleland concluded a series of lectures on preaching by attempting to describe the kind of believer sermons are supposed to create. Unwittingly, he described the kind of believer who creates the best sermons. And unerringly he revealed the secret of Charles Kraemer. For he was the believer who walked in the world "as a sympathetic stranger in an alien land," knowing all the while that the world was not for him. He was "ready to help its inhabitants in love," and for him success and failure were only by-products: the real job, the job in which he had his joy, was witness. He sowed as well as he could, leaving to God the responsibility of any increases.

Thus (the believer) works with the strain off. It is sometimes wise to remember that there is such a thing as Christian nonchalance. Maybe there is room for a new beatitude: "Blessed are the debonair," in

62

whom the Word of God sparkles with graciousness and charm.

Blessed are the debonair, and twice blessed are those who walk through this alien land in the company of the debonair.

Farewell, courageous friend. Thanks be to God for sharing you with us.